STRAIGHT AHEAD, AS USUAL

Education Reforms Put Simply

Logan Patrick Harrison

authorHOUSE™

AuthorHouse™
1663 Liberty Drive
Bloomington, IN 47403
www.authorhouse.com
Phone: 1-800-839-8640

First published by AuthorHouse   1/4/2010

ISBN: 978-1-4490-6141-8 (e)
ISBN: 978-1-4490-6140-1 (sc)
ISBN: 978-1-4490-7274-2 (hc)

Library of Congress Control Number: 2009913964

Printed in the United States of America
Bloomington, Indiana

This book is printed on acid-free paper.

In Loving Memory of Jean M. Harrison

July 21, 1934 – August 9, 1990

PREFACE AND ACKNOWLEDGEMENTS

This book does not necessarily represent the view of any of the former or current elected officials, my employer(s), athletes, coaches, business leaders, civic leaders, or any organization or group of which I am affiliated. I did not interview or interact with any of the people mentioned for the purposes of this book, and it is solely based upon my own research, thoughts, and opinions.

I wrote this book in order to present a short analysis of why states all across the country need education reform, and why we in Indiana have an opportunity to be at the forefront. I felt that it was important to be short and concise because many of the working families for whom these proposals would benefit most do not have the time to read a large book, and it is people like us who need these reforms the most.

This is going to take a joint effort to overcome these obstacles to education reform by individuals from all walks of life. It is my hope that all of you will join this effort and recognize the urgency of this situation in which we face. In one way or another, it affects us all. I make no claim in this book to be an expert in anything, but I do have common sense, and I did experience this firsthand. We will not all agree on the details of the implementation of some of these policies, but it is my hope that we will agree that it is crucial to no longer continue to do the same thing and expect a different outcome.

I would like to thank my best friend, Jennifer L. Prinz, for her hard work in helping me edit this book. I owe special thanks to my Mother, Linda J. Harrison-George, for always encouraging me to be the very best that I could be, and to stand up for myself and others. Finally, I would like to thank the following who not only attended school with me much of my life, but whose lifelong friendships have taught me so much: W. Scott Laham, Kyle A. Miller, Kevin P. Murphy, Nicholas A. Sons, and David J. Stadtmiller.

CHAPTER 1: STANDING STILL

"Education is not the means of showing people how to get what they want. Education is an exercise by means of which enough men, it is hoped, will learn to want what is worth having."

President Ronald W. Reagan

The First Time Around

I began writing this book in the fall of 2003. It was my second to last semester in college. Originally, the idea for this book was a "how to" succeed guide geared to first generation college students. The basis of this idea stemmed from the fact that all three of my roommates and I came from similar backgrounds: single-parent households and the first in our immediate families to attend college. In my particular instance, my father attended and graduated from the University of Cincinnati after a tour in the United States Army. However, his presence was non-existent, and I was raised almost entirely by my mother and her family. Thus, considering myself a first generation college student, I noticed a pattern of similar questions, concerns, and strengths we all had.

Five years after graduation from Indiana University, the same idea evolved from the how to succeed as a first generation college student guide to a why first generation college students should organize and demand a competitive education market and an overhaul of the primary and secondary education model because it is outmoded and defunct. I want this book to be a challenge to educate others that the current education model, and those that vigorously advocate for it, are just plain wrong. A grass roots initiative is imperative. Otherwise, the quality of our higher education is going to suffer, or become education facilities for foreign students to come learn.[1] With an overhaul, it is my opinion that negative patterns can be effectively addressed and an educational market can be formed so that competition will govern the best solutions and arbitrary, ineffective regulations that thwart innovation will be eliminated.

In my first weeks at Indiana University Bloomington ("IUB"), I was in awe with the diverse student body. Of the approximately 37,000 undergraduate and graduate students at IUB, approximately 9%-10% were international students. As a young man barely eighteen years of age, it fascinated me that people came from all over the world to go to school with me. This was the very beginning of the twenty-first century and President Clinton used the term globalization quite a bit, but people like me had no idea what it really meant. We certainly did not comprehend the impact it would have on our education and, more importantly, our careers.

A few things struck me about the foreign students: their absence from remedial courses, their comfort with technology, their work ethic, and their absence from campus computer labs. For example, I was in Kirkwood Hall at IUB where varying liberal arts and introductory courses were held during my freshman year. A remedial English writing class consisted almost entirely of American students. I thought this to be a bit embarrassing for our country since English is primarily our first language. I was not embarrassed of the students themselves but that our schools had failed these students, and foreign students who did not speak English as their primary language tested out of the course.

Then, I immediately wondered about remedial math courses. Math seems to be tough for a lot of people. Sure enough there were no foreign students in the particular course I observed either. American universities have superior higher education institutions, but our primary and secondary institutions have some serious flaws. To me, remedial courses at the collegiate level are troubling by their very nature because they are a waste of time, resources, and money. By definition, one is not getting their money's worth of his or her college education, but, rather, learning at a higher level what they should've learned in our primary or secondary institutions.

Another observance was the computer labs. I noticed all of them were populated primarily by African-American students. The other students usually just used the computer labs to print documents. For those students who used the computer lab for their primary computer at college, it was clear they likely did not grow up with one at home.

Therefore, they were not likely educated on how to exploit the advantages and necessities associated with computers that were required for the business school, word processing, programming, and many other skills that were not only convenient but also becoming a minimum requirement for employment.

None of the foreign students I observed were facing these obstacles, and their comfort level with technology was objectively superior to a good number of American students. I primarily observed this through many core classes required by the Kelly School of Business, like Excel courses, Access, and a website design class.

Finally, many foreign students' work ethics amazed me. It was constant. I saw their hunger for success. This quality is also strong with first generation college students and middle-class students. As first generation college students, my roommates and I seemed to be driven by ambition, competition, and a desire to be successful. Like many of the foreign students whose families encouraged them to attend American universities, our parents and grandparents pushed and supported us to attend college, to learn, to come home and contribute to our local communities, and to have a better and more prosperous life.

Like the foreign students, I felt my roommates and I were independent. We were in charge of our tuition, financial livelihood, and had to be hard workers during the summer months and during the school year to supplement our tuition and living expenses. It forced time management, responsibility, real life experiences, struggles, perseverance, and good people skills. Similarly, many of the foreign students were far away from home. Sometimes so far, they would not return home for a few years at a time. Being abroad undoubtedly forces independence.

Thus, it became one of my goals to write this book and show others how to capitalize on all the abovementioned characteristics that generally makes one successful. These characteristics include improving technological skills and access, math, communication, and writing skills. These skills are the foundation of almost every newly created job today.

From my perspective as a first generation college student, I felt that the biggest disadvantage for first generation college students' parents and the student himself or herself was that they knew something was not working at the primary and secondary education level, but they did not know what to demand as an alternative or how to demand it. More importantly, they did not know why one alternative would increase educational success more than another. But how could they? Those in charge of creating the education model are usually politically appointed bureaucrats or are hired to create or thwart a specific agenda. Meanwhile polices created are ineffective, but unfortunately may appear to most people as legitimate.

The education system is dominated by powerful teachers unions that largely dictate the model, and there is no counter-lobby to advocate for the interests of the parents and students. At least, there is no effective organization that can rival the massive teachers' unions lobby. Furthermore, these powerful unions largely dominate the media and convolute the outcome, and it is hard to tell what we should demand to improve the model. One purpose in writing this book is to expose some inequities in our education system and inspire others to create just that balance. We need a parents' and students' union, or its equivalent.

The Middle-Class

I am not sure that I truly knew what the term middle-class meant until recently. I did know, from The World is Flat by Thomas L. Friedman, that according to the U.S. Census done once every ten years a large number of people consider themselves middle-class, and some of those people probably aren't. Friedman wrote that the middle-class is a state of mind. It is "hope" to improve your wealth, contribution to society, and most importantly the lives of the succeeding generation in your own family.[2]

It also occurred to me that my family was at many points likely part of those people that checked the "middle-class" box, and we probably didn't always fall in the governmental margin for middle-class – whatever that may be. However, our ambition and pride helped make us middle-class. In fact, without hope, we would have been considered poor. My family had a lot of hope because we had personal responsibilities and drives to do the best we could. Thus, I agree – the middle-class is largely a state of mind, but one that defines the American culture to its core. The middle-class is the team that everyone cheers loudly for to achieve something better for themselves.

From the formation of this country, America was considered an underdog. We were not supposed to prevail over the British for our independence in the Revolutionary War, but we did. One can find evidence that Americans love to root for the underdog countless times, from the Revolutionary War to how we root for our sports teams. In fact, Americans are at their best when we're portrayed that way. I equate those of us in the middle-class as underdogs. We don't always have all the resources and tools as the "big dogs," but usually we have more heart. That's why so often we end up winning. More importantly, we don't give up easily. If we were people that gave in easily, there would be no more Chicago Cubs fans.

Hometown Favorite

My home state, Indiana, is considered the heart of basketball country. One of Indiana's famous underdog examples, nationally memorialized in the 1986 movie *Hoosiers*, is the famous 1954 Milan High School basketball team's victory over Muncie Central. Many times around the family kitchen table, I heard my mom's brother, Uncle Mike, fondly discuss this story, and his recount of listening to the game on the radio and celebrating the legendary underdog victory.

With an enrollment of only 161 students, Milan High School was the smallest school ever to win a single-class state basketball title in Indiana. In 1954, unlike most states, Indiana held a single-class tournament where all schools in the state competed for the same championship in one of America's largest and most popular high school tournaments. Thus, a David and Goliath match-up was possible. The Hoosier state thrived on the competition. In fact, this love for the game caused a lot of controversy in 1997 when the Indiana High School Athletic Association decided to organize the high schools according to classes based on student enrollment.

This is an example so near and dear to Hoosiers' hearts that then Indiana gubernatorial candidate Mitch Daniels launched his 2004 campaign out of Milan High School's victory site at Butler University's Hinkle Field House. He wanted to invoke the Hoosier voters with our history and themes of triumph against all odds.

Prior to 2004, Indiana was a state where all levels were standing still. It needed an injection of new ideas to encourage competition for jobs, a better educated citizenry, and overall sense of optimism. Thus, now Governor Daniels, known for bold changes in my state, likened Indiana to Milan High School because it was underrated, underdeveloped, but, most importantly, underestimated. His choice to launch his campaign at the field house poised the voters to give him a chance to lead the state like Coach Marvin Wood did for the Milan High School basketball team. Like Coach Wood, Mitch Daniels wanted to force Hoosiers to aim higher, think boldly, and seek a positive energy from those who thought this state couldn't do any better.

If that doesn't capture the energy needed to overhaul the current educational model and create an environment cheering for our underdog students, then perhaps my most recent favorite will. It was during the 2008 Summer Olympics in Beijing, China in the 4x100 freestyle relay with Michael Phelps and Jason Lezak. I don't know this for sure, but I had an immediate hunch while watching it live that night exactly what the French swimmers did wrong.

The French prior to the start of the race were speaking of how they were going to "smash" the Americans because of the French men's favorability in this race and overall superior training and talent. This continued right on up to the start of the race. It is my understanding that the French were indeed the better swimmers for this race. Where did they make their mistake? They continued to fire up the Americans and remind our great swimmers they were the underdog. I immediately said to my girlfriend, Jenny, that it was a mistake.

In a split second, Lezak glided into the gold medal because we Americans thrive on being the underdog. Moreover, we thrive on being taunted as the underdog. The French swimmers would have been better off keeping their mouths shut. Therefore, I welcome having core values stirred a bit in a healthy fashion. It sets off nerves that our opponents wished hadn't been set off.[3]

Stating the Obvious

Sometimes things just need to be said. The elephant in the room is so often never directly mentioned in our debates: let's not start by making that same mistake. Parents who are well educated have children that perform well on test scores and in school in general.[4] Policy makers from Washington, D.C. all the way to our local school boards think that it is primarily because the difference in wealth status.

Government leaders' solutions are always to throw more money at the problem, or at least pledge to increase the education budget for that very philosophy. Increasing a budget in this instance often just enables schools to expand facilities, which increases overall operating expenses and, thus, less money flows directly to the students. This "solution" also is a good way for politicians to cover up the real problems. If the money is going to fund the same old educational model, then the majority of Americans do not expect a different outcome; we just expect more wasted tax dollars to fund something that is fundamentally outdated and failing to create competitive human capital for a global economy.

Undoubtedly, income discrepancies and "social statuses" all play a role, but the actual root of the problem is parents who are uneducated, undereducated, or poorly educated know less about how the classroom works on all levels of education from kindergarten to higher education. Therefore, they are unable to be consumers and demand any different for themselves or, more importantly, for their children. That is the heart of the problem. This is no easy task to remedy, and teachers' unions, stale philosophies, and regulations that euthanize innovation and divert resources make it all the more challenging. However, this current education model cripples middle-class salaries, continues to increase poverty, and wastes human intellect.

Good schooling must be the foundation in order to have a legitimate start at improving the problem. A *New York Times* article about one's IQ suggests that with the mere presence of education, one's IQ can raise and decline– even over the summer months when American children are on vacation and out of the classroom.[5] Good schooling correlates with higher IQs.[6]

This study is not a revelation that can improve the lives of millions of people because those students attending good schools are more likely to have educated parents with high IQs, and it is well established that IQ is largely inherited. However, there are signs that IQ can be raised within a margin. Alternatively, IQ can fall or remain stagnant if educational techniques are not stimulating the brain.

Thus, good schooling should be available to all so that intellect can be maximized. There is no telling how many children there are left on the cusp of being considered below average to average or average to above average intelligence. Good schooling will make the difference of them being college graduates or working in a place that they are, in effect, underemployed with little capability of moving beyond the hole that American elementary and secondary education has put them into for reasons that will be laid out in the following chapters.

The American Education Model

The current American education model plays a large role in driving this disparity between the middle-class and the wealthy. The current American model consists of a curriculum not far removed from one designed to prepare young American children for the industrial revolution. Many private schools have more rigorous curriculums, and more "electives" that spur innovation and creativity. Nonetheless, they are still regulated by the states, and private schools have to adhere to arcane accreditation standards, which are often a waste of time and resources.

In contrast, public schools at the least are preparing children for the bare minimum. In other words, they are preparing American children for jobs that largely don't exist anymore: manufacturing jobs.[7] This model worked and worked well for many years from its inception through post World War II. By the 1970s, it needed revamping. The world was getting smaller because of technology, and by the 1980s government reports were beginning to read "Crisis Ahead for Our Children."

The ongoing failure to revamp this model has had a disproportionate impact on the middle-class and poor. It is certainly more challenging for these two factions of society to send their children to private schools, to be well versed in how the classroom should operate, or probably most common, to have the time to commit to making a change because of the economic necessity of working one or multiple jobs. Thus, these demographics have fallen faster behind, have increasingly experienced stagnant wages, unemployment risks, and have been underemployed.[8]

The whole point of educating our children is to prepare them to function and compete in a civil society, and to prepare them to obtain a job to provide for themselves and possibly future children of their own. Fortune favors the prepared mind, however.[9] We need to ensure that our students are not just doing any homework, but the right kind of homework.[10] Moreover, curriculums need to hone in on weaknesses and provide both supplemental and reinforcement exercises. To put it simply, primary and secondary graduation credits need to focus on turning those education credits into cash.

The goal is to create as many untouchables as possible, or people whose jobs cannot be outsourced, digitized, or automated.[11] The new world is now more than ever about being able to operate in, mobilize, inspire, and manage a multi-dimensional and multicultural workforce.[12] It is imperative that schools be given the freedom to hone in on weak subjects, and outsource stronger subjects to the home and to the individual student via technology.

The number of jobs that require math, science, and engineering skills is growing at about a 5% rate per year.[13] The number of Americans in the eighteen to twenty-four year old demographic who receive science degrees has fallen to seventeenth in the world, whereas just three years ago Americans ranked third.[14] The foundational skills required to enter these fields are usually American children's weakest points across the board throughout primary and secondary education.

The Perfect Storm

Now is the time to reform education. Use this extraordinary recession to demand a difference as you retrain for new jobs through education, prepare your children for a competitive trade, and turn the page on an outdated model. Institutions are resistant to change unless it can be shown that its operating model is in deep trouble, and it needs to do something to survive.[15]

Although economically painful, this might be the perfect storm – for education reform anyway. As I write, hundreds of thousands of jobs are being lost, and many of them will not be replaced even with a turnaround which will undoubtedly happen. New jobs will be created, but these jobs will continue to require new skill sets, different types of training, and new approaches. In other words, many workers – as quite a few already have – will be heading back to the classrooms to learn what was not taught to them the first time around, brush up on things they have forgotten, and be retrained for completely new careers.

Many coincidentally will be heading back to school with their children, or they will be preceding their children just slightly. It will expose two generations simultaneously to learn how the classroom works, and to demand better quality of education for their dollars. The elder generation experiencing the discrepancy will want to force things to be better for their children and themselves.

Indeed the perfect storm for education reform might be upon us, and it would be unthinkable to waste it. We can no longer afford to continue to educate the middle-class under a 1940s and 1950s model, and expect them to be prepared for a completely different economic environment.

Feels like Today

I was born during a severe but briefer economic recession. The year after I was born, the Reagan Administration's National Commission on Excellence in Education published *A Nation at Risk*. This report indicated that despite our major accomplishments, i.e., putting a man on the moon, the nation's education system was declining at alarming levels. For instance, in nineteen different international tests Americans were not first or second, but on seven we were last. Thirteen percent of seventeen year olds and twenty-three million Americans were functionally illiterate and 40% of minorities were functionally illiterate. Finally, 25% of college math courses were remedial and teaching the same coursework being taught in high school.[16] Thus, the nation was officially put on notice in 1983 that the educational model had broken down.

It is my understanding that the Reagan Administration had been the first in many years to recognize the 1940s educational model was not sustainable if America wanted to continue to be a world power. However, it was still pre-globalization for the most part so the sense of urgency did not reveal the international competition like it does today. Thus, the potential crisis was recognized, but the actuality of the crisis could not ignite the spark it would take to overhaul and bring true reform. So in the meantime, Washington and many states just continued to pledge more money to this model, and it did little to change what was being learned, how it was being learned, and to create a market for ideas to compete and evolve into a model that is fit for a global economy.

Meanwhile, India and China began evolving into superpowers, and have implemented educational standards that reflect future success for their citizens much more than America's today. Over two decades have passed and four additional U.S. Presidents have served in the White

House, since President Reagan's *A Nation in Crisis* report was issued. Things are worse, however, not better.

So, let me be clear: we are currently not expected to be able to compete on the same level with Asian nations and continue as the economic superpower within the next twenty years. India and China are just doing it, and making it happen. Their leaders have chosen to remain silent about the issue because they don't want to taunt us Americans as the underdog. It will disrupt their plans as you can see with the abovementioned stories.

We need to shroud ourselves in themes that we are now the underdog and create a model that enables us to healthily compete with them, or we can continue an outmoded system and begin to warm up to the idea that we are going to work for them. I would prefer the former, and I think you do too.

Let's organize, and let's get to work!

Chapter 2: Play the Hand Your Dealt

"All of you can turn learning into an adventure. And to do this you have to prepare not just by studying, but by studying hard, especially math and science. . . ."
President George H. W. Bush

This chapter is more autobiographical than the rest, but it is important to establish that I am not chiseling on stones and throwing these accusations from a glass house. It is imperative that the following be told to establish where I came from and the people along the way that I saw left behind. This chapter will stress the importance of active parenting in education and how perceived disadvantages can be capitalized on to make one a well rounded individual at an early age. It also emphasizes the importance of the community one lives in, and how there is always a learning experience in each and every community.

By far, I am not the first to overcome challenging situations. In fact, I feel I have accomplished relatively nothing that I should not have to date. In comparison to many others, I had it easy but still different. This country has no shortage of success stories by individuals who came from humble beginnings and achieved extraordinary things. This short background is but a glimpse of the advantages I was given to get thus far.

As we all likely agree from the last chapter, Americans thrive on the stories of average people doing extraordinary things. What many people do not realize is many of the extraordinary people I write about in the following chapter are not known outside of their small community. I am sure you can rattle off the names of similar kinds of people in yours because these personalities are everywhere. Very few are what would be considered famous, but certainly they are the type of people that built this country and pushed many of the rest of us to strive to do extraordinary things.

Some Basics That Will Always Apply

I deserve no recognition or commendation for doing what is or was right to this point, and in my opinion no one else does either. One is supposed to grow up, be responsible, be the best he or she can be, and contribute a little, not because he or she is forced to but because it is the right thing to do. That's a sound philosophy to start with and keeps you on track.

For me, as a child, complaining wasn't allowed. My Aunt Jean's ("G.G." as I called her for short) motto when times were tough was, "Someone always had it worse than you, and you do with what you have at the time." Because she had a hand in rearing me, I was taught to make do with the resources I had and find a way to make it work. This rule sparked innovation and creativity, and it forced me to maximize the resources I had.

My life under Aunt Jean's philosophy instigated a philosophy of my own. I consider myself a very blessed person. However, like many other blessed people, I have always felt an obligation to help others in my community seek the tools and advice necessary so that they may reach their goals. It is up to them from there. It was that simple philosophy that grounded me not all that long ago, and not all that far away from where I live now.

Never Far From Home

I was born in 1982 on the 1200 block of South Rural Street on Indianapolis' near eastside. I briefly mentioned in the previous chapter that the state of Indiana has always been an underdog state. Likewise, Indianapolis, its capital, also struggles to gain recognition as a leading competitor on the nation's map.

Indianapolis, nicknamed "Naptown" for its uneventful perception, is topographically spread out. Yet, perceptions can be deceiving because experiencing my neighborhood in the right way was definitely eventful and could make you a fairly well-rounded person. Perhaps it was not in ways that one might prefer, but it is better than having not lived or to have lived under the guise of naiveté.

My family moved to the eastside of Indianapolis circa 1959 in the St. Phillip Neri Parish neighborhood located just a little farther south on Rural Street, the same street I was born. At the time of my mother's family's arrival on the near eastside, the area and parish was predominantly working-class, Irish-Catholic families. Many never ventured far outside their neighborhoods besides military deployments, and most returned to the eastside to raise or rejoin their families, whatever the reason for their absence. My family was no different.

Eastside residents' priorities were probably not all that different from other urban communities throughout America. They included their families, their work, their parish, Notre Dame Football, and the Cathedral Irish or Scecina Crusaders. The latter two were two Catholic high schools that served many of the east deanery Catholic grade schools. These two schools usually had excellent football programs, and were sources of great pride for the neighborhood, and rivalries for the other schools in the area. These priorities may have varied in any particular order from household-to-household, but it is a close representation.

The typical professional make-up of my block was cops, firefighters, bar owners or bar workers, factory laborers, truck drivers, and construction workers. Usually, the formally educated people in our community were the school teachers, the priests, and other clergy.

My mother reminds me that the eastside I was born into wasn't all that different from 1959 and she's right. By the time I was born in 1982, the above description was still pretty accurate. There were more characters among us, for lack of a better description. She said there was always people in the neighborhood that you kept your children away from, neighborhood drunks, and those that had little pride or incentive to take care of their property. Although these residents were the minority, they usually provided the free entertainment from one's front porch, the majority of the police runs, and, unfortunately, the proliferation that eventually resulted in the near eastside's demise. Nonetheless, it was and still is considered home to me.

My Best Teachers: The Role of Parenting, the Family, Tradition, and the Community

From the time I was an infant, I was read to by someone on a daily basis at the least. I was taught to write at home, and, most importantly, I was taught to be a leader in the home. It was important to stand up for yourself if you thought you were right, and to stand up for others that couldn't stand up for themselves. In his book, *The World is Flat*, Thomas

L. Friedman writes, "[e]ducation begins in a home where reading is intrinsically valuable and necessary; where recognition of the hard work associated with education and doing well in school are top priorities; and where parents join schools in having high expectations for their children's success."[17]

Parents partnering with educators on middle-class to low-income families are, however, dwindling.[18] Some may argue that is because these parents have to work more because their incomes have not risen with inflation and other costs. That is a very compelling argument, and after reading this book hopefully you will see the need to reorganize the American education model because it is at the heart of the income disparity. Whatever the case may be, teachers need a partner in the home, and the parents need qualified teachers in the school.

It is hard for any parent to accomplish all that life demands while also reinforcing and teaching additional basic educational skills in the home. Looking back, I now realize that sentiment more than ever. I was raised by a single parent juggling two full time jobs: nursing and me. Children raised by single-parents, however, also can gain many practical skills and leadership. Although I am not advocating whatsoever for single parenthood, growing up in a single-parent home can be a positive experience in the long run because of some of the challenges we face early on growing up in such a situation.

Children who are raised by single parents would likely agree that at times it is also a companion type relationship. You have to be more responsible because there is less money, and you have to be more mature and stay at home alone at an earlier age because there is no longer any money for a sitter. All children depend on their parents in some fashion, but with single parent households the parent has to depend on the children for it to work. If a child fails their single parent, he or she has impacted the small, immediate family in a significant way.

On my end, I had to help run a household. That meant taking on the role that in some cases would have been filled by a grown man at a young age. I came to see these things had to be done in order for our small family to work. I depended on it and my mom depended on it.

We often had to hustle to get everything accomplished. Yet even though I may have been more mature for my age than most, I still had child like tendencies. I was easily distracted, I watched people, and I investigated things just like any curious, young boy would when exploring his surroundings. I had to go the grocery store, and any other miscellaneous shopping to help get groceries for the week. My mother would have to constantly remind me that it was important to be on time, important to stay on task, and important to keep moving along.

To do this she would sternly say, while trying to keep me on task in public, "Straight ahead son, as usual." She knew there was little time in the day to waste, but it's tough to get that through to a kid because there are just too many appealing distractions to take you off course. We still had a lot to do, and the grocery store or other errand shopping was just one thing. The house needed to be cleaned, I had sports practice, and I had either school work or some project to complete on any given day.

In comparison to many single parents, my mother was lucky and had a lot of help, including her three older sisters and her oldest brother. My aunts' and uncle's children were raised, and they all took an active interest in how I turned out. Besides my mother's brother Jimmy who was deceased by the time I was born, I was closer than most nieces or nephews to each one of my mother's siblings ranging from birth to now.

In particular, my Mother's eldest sibling, Jean who I called "G.G.", owned the duplex where my mother lived when I was born on south Rural Street. It was a white, two-story house with living quarters, a kitchen, two bedrooms, and a full bath on each side of the house. My mother and I lived on one side of the duplex and Jean on the other side. My mother is one of six children: Jean, Rita Lou, Anna "Jo," Michael, James "Jimmy," and Linda (my mother). Jean predominantly raised my mother and her next to oldest brother Jimmy because she was fifteen years her senior, and her mother and father had other issues by the time they latter two children were coming of age. As a result, Jean never married and devoted her entire life to her siblings and her siblings' children.

Rita, Anna, and Michael had children that were comparable in ages to each other, but their children were eighteen to twenty-five years my senior, and my first cousins. My mother's siblings were a good bit older than my mother, and some of Rita, Anna, and Michael's children were just a few years my mother's junior. She was an aunt, for example, for the first time at eight. This had a profound effect on the way I turned out because I was predominantly always around adults in the early years. I was much more inclined to act much older than I actually was because

I grew up hearing about the World War II years, its impact, and effect on the country from those of the age who were of the Korean War era. It destined me to be an old soul.

Jean's short but large impact on my life played an even larger role. Jean played a matriarchal role for the whole family. She commanded a respect that she did not insist upon, but most gave it to her. She solved problems, gave financial assistance, a place to live, and someone to talk to when you had no one else. She was a true leader within her family and in her community.

Jean, having no biological children of her own, and never having married considered me a grandson, and at the beginning of my life we either lived next to Jean or with her. She watched me while my mom worked, and we were, in effect, inseparable.

As a small child, she was much like what I wanted to become in some form. Adults who think children do not observe their behavior and actions couldn't be more wrong. I always admired that she was the one everyone came to see. I noticed that some would act differently out of respect, and they did not want to do anything to disappoint her.

She made decisions calmly and without haste, was conservative with her money, always had a very neat and clean appearance, and took pride in all her tasks. Most of all she was always someone that people came to for advice. Jean was also a devout Catholic, and was the type of person to rise early and go to bed late. She kept an immaculate house and would always tell me not being clean about yourself and/ or your surroundings was inexcusable. She would say, "You don't have to have money to be clean." It was her way of saying: always be prideful about where you came from, how people perceived you, and who was watching. Otherwise, how were you ever to improve?

Jean was often the one who picked me up and took me to school in the early years. After I would get into the car, she would want to know what I accomplished that day, and what we were working on. She was interested in not only what I learned, but how it was being taught to me, and who it was that was teaching it. It was important for her that I attend Catholic school, but it was more important to her that I was learning the right skills. In some of the advantages that private schools bring to the table as opposed to publicly run schools, she was likely more concerned with me learning about my religion, getting disciplined appropriately, and being part of a larger faith-based community.

For example, one afternoon, after a snack, I had gotten home from the second grade at St. Therese the Little Flower. Jean and I sat down to review my math homework. Interactive post-school work was a priority with Jean whether it was formal home-work or a hands-on engagement on what was going on in school so that we could review it together in case there were further questions.

On one particular afternoon, Jean was concerned about two things: I had too many eraser marks on my page and I was using my fingers to count. The eraser marks concerned her because I was answering without thinking, meaning there was something I didn't understand. She felt that I should've thought longer and harder before making a hasty decision and, more importantly, that I needed to conceptually understand why it was the answer. Also, I needed to make sure to ask if I didn't understand something, and then sit and go over it until I did. If she could, she would give a real-life scenario of why it was important for me to know this or that depending on what we were working on that afternoon.

Another example had to do with me using my fingers to count to get the answers to my math homework. This method concerned her because I was depending on an inefficient method. In her mind, how was I going to get a job during high school and college if I couldn't make change? Never mind it was the beginning of the age of electronic cash registers. What if they went down during my shift? Thus, she put it in her terms when thinking about basic math: think in groups of tens. This helped me to understand the concept, but it taught me to always ask or find out why something is done the way it is, and to not make decisions in haste. Further, it taught me not to be dependent on something that may fail.

Jean was not, however, a formally educated teacher. In fact, she had retired from an assembly line at Western Electric, which was the manufacturing arm of AT&T. She understood the importance of education for my generation, and she wanted more than anything for me to be competitive. She understood the importance of it for my generation not because it was less important for her generation or even my mother's, but because the market was changing and she saw that the new market didn't just need more service based skills; it demanded it. For the early 1980s, Jean was keenly aware of the shift from manufacturing jobs to service based jobs.

Indeed she was right; Western Electric dissolved its operations in Indianapolis on her thirtieth year of service in 1986 to the company. It was just in time for her pension to vest, but she was always mindful of those that were not lucky enough for that to happen. It was now even more imperative for her to teach me to be adaptable and prepare myself for a world of ever adapting change. She also taught me not be at the mercy of someone else because I had failed to see nuances evolve.

Jean did this not because she likely wanted a less labor intensive and more rewarding job for me, but she knew I would not have much more of a choice. She understood change, adapted to it, didn't complain about it, and focused on the people who were less fortunate before feeling sorry for herself, whatever the challenge. She insisted I have the same attitude about change.

Eight Years Old Going on Thirty

Jean died in August 1990 at the relatively young age of fifty-six from lung cancer. I had just turned eight years old. That was a big change for me. The anchor for our little family and our entire extended family was no longer present for our day-to-day lives. She had given me the tools not only to survive but also to succeed without her. I picked them up and used them albeit probably in a less gentle and charismatic way.

Jean left my mother and me everything. With that, we moved farther east in Indianapolis to a nice ranch house and a more stable neighborhood. It was 1990, and the St. Phillip Neri Parish my family had lived in on and off for thirty years had dwindled into one of the more crime infested areas of the whole city. Sadly, it remains that way today.

I continued to go to St. Therese the Little Flower Catholic School, and life was pretty good. Although I have confidence that I still had a good chance to turn out well, it might have been even harder without "G.G." It was bizarre to not have Jean around anymore to say the least, but I continued to try and live how she lived or at least think via her philosophies. At eight it was instilled in me that no matter what you have to deal with in life, somebody else out there always had it worse. Jean left me big tasks for an eight year old to fill, but it was much easier to adhere to tasks than to fill her shoes.

Chapter 3: The State
of Our Classrooms

"In this new land, education will be every citizen's most prized possession."

President William J. Clinton

The state of our classrooms is outmoded for a global economy.[19] There are political barriers, poor economic incentives for teachers, misallocation of resources, onerous regulations, and little focus on education basics that are essential to being competitive in this economy. All of this thwarts innovation and creativity by teachers and students.

Reorganizing our education model is critical because the world we live in is becoming increasingly technologically advanced, meaning so many tasks are digitized and done electronically.[20] Creativity and innovation is highly valued in the global economy. We must create an educational environment for our students that makes them versatile and provides our children with more sustainable skills. The ultimate goal is to arm our children with these skills, enable them to use these skills in a larger market, and encourage them to be creative. It is important to first understand what factors drive the current American model before we are able to see how these same factors stand in the way of a more ideal and a better model.

Political Power

Political power is usually what drives the model of any institution. Education is not immune. Teachers' unions in many states are powerful political lobbies who largely dictate the model of how classrooms are organized. Public school teachers are economically and politically pressured to join these unions. For example, the union dues in Indiana are withheld directly from teachers' pay who join these unions. This money collected from teachers all across the state is then used to fund state and federal legislators' campaigns, marketing, and teachers' association staff members to monitor, lobby, draft, and influence legislation. In turn, legislators insert all sorts of rules and regulations into bills that help guard the unions' initiatives: protecting the government monopoly on education and providing teachers with job security.

There is nothing illegal about how all of this works. In fact, it is a constitutional right to lobby your legislature, contribute money to lobbying efforts, and for the candidates to accept money for their political campaigns. However, candidates that accept money from these teachers unions better be prepared to do what the union wants when it comes time for legislative votes that affect its interests. If the representatives don't, then the unions will cut off the donations as quickly as they contributed it to them.

Obviously, this points out for all intents and purposes that it is the unions that have the ultimate control, and it is the unions that dictate the policy that decides school funding, uniform wages for teachers based on seniority, and licensing credentials. As you can see, teachers' unions represent the teachers and no one else.

Our country needs to be education consumers and to demand a choice for education; if not, teachers unions will dominate the policy debate and its implementation. The unions have louder voices, not just because they have the money, but because we have allowed them to control the debate, dictate the policy, and give primary and secondary education in America a slow death, taking all the future human capital with it. There needs to be parents' and students' unions. As parents and students, we need to drive the debate and change the direction of the policy.

Perceptively Good, but Misguided Populist Arguments

A popular political argument that union representatives make on behalf of teachers is that education consumers cannot measure what teachers do for a living.[21] This argument is meant to highlight the important influences teachers can have on one's life. The argument exists to persuade our society that performance standards are not necessary and teachers do not have objective indicators that are measurable.

If wholly believed, this argument is dangerous. Like all other jobs, teachers provide a service and their success or failure can very much be measured and quantified. They are preparing future human capital to produce an economic benefit in the real world. It is true that it is likely immeasurable or unquantifiable for a third grade teacher to measure the impact of their science experiment that initially inspired a couple of young future physicians in their class. Things like that undoubtedly happen, and it is immeasurable. However, we can measure where a student is in comparison to his peers, and where he or she needs to be in order to compete in the future. Students' performance is quantifiable.

Success by teachers in underprivileged neighborhoods should be rewarded even more because they have a harder challenge. It is the equivalent of a CEO turning around a troubled company. The argument that this education achievement is unquantifiable is a mere protectionist argument made by unions to protect job security as opposed to retaining it based on results.

More Union Protections

Unions are not misrepresenting to parents or children that they also represent their interests because after all they are called teachers unions. For one to think they have anyone else in their interests with regard to the educational model is absurd. In order to achieve their legislative goals and influence regulations, unions bargain for a contract with school districts on behalf of all teachers. These unions bargain for wages, stifle competition from other educational choices, bargain for pensions, healthcare benefits, and a whole nuance of policy initiatives to protect public schools from competition. To understand why we need to revamp our educational model it is important to focus on the unions' influence with teachers' wages and competition, and why unions do everything in their power to thwart wages and competition.

The teachers' unions' most important job is to protect jobs for the teachers that pay into the union. A common and all too often typical example of this was when Indianapolis Public Schools (IPS) decided to fire 300 newly hired teachers in early 2009. Job security with many teachers' unions' contracts is solely based on seniority.[22] Thus, if you have been at a school for twenty-two years and perform poorly that is irrelevant to the analysis of whether or not a teacher is fired. In fact, that teacher is likely retained. By contrast, the teacher who has been employed for two years and performing excellently is laid off. If the opposite result occurred, it would be a violation of the labor contract between the teachers' unions and the school district. In fact, in the 2009 IPS situation, the pink-slipped teachers included nine of the thirty-two teachers recently announced as IPS' teacher of the year nominees. Two of the ten finalists for the district wide honor were laid off.[23]

Such a policy misaligns the incentive based model on work and performance standards. If there is little incentive to achieve positive results because of misaligned rewards, then it is hard to implement performance based standards and nearly impossible to measure results. If merely gaining seniority over colleagues is all that drives competition among one's peers, there will be less innovation and desire to think outside the box to improve the education model.

In the abovementioned example, the newer teachers had the freshest ideas, the most recent exposure to technological initiatives to aid them in the classroom, and an even greater sense of contemporary challenges.

However, none of these strengths or weaknesses was taken into account in the ultimate decision of whom to fire because a predetermined union contract provided for this remedy. The school corporation was forced to agree to the union's decision on how a layoff would be handled. The end result of the union contract was devastating for our students when the effect of its provisions was carried out.

Government Schools

The second biggest job of unions is making sure that public schools maintain a monopoly, and thwart the proliferation of all competing schools as much as they can.[24] Former Indianapolis Mayor Stephen Goldsmith across the board championed government that also competed with the private sector, and emphasized the importance of this competition for public schools as well throughout his tenure as mayor.

Although former Mayor Goldsmith was exactly right about school monopolies, he emphasized this during a time when the national economy and state economy was doing relatively well and the disparities produced by this outdated education model for the labor market in a globalized economy were not as apparent yet. Therefore, it was harder to incite the necessary political will to create change. Business as usual in the general assembly went on without regard to education reform. Globalization was real, but not recognized in everyone's daily life yet, unlike today.

Competing educational models cannot come without demand from customers. In order to have actual choices, customers must demand a market and then innovation will follow from the market.[25] Public schools in Indiana insulate themselves from customers though. For example, most school board elections are held during primary elections, when the least amount of people vote. By doing so, public schools protect themselves from any true change or having to run on any platform other than getting the necessary few people they know to come to the polls and vote for them.[26] In other words, it is a big game of hiding the ball, combined with parents who are misled about what to shop for when it comes to preparing their son or daughter for a decent education to prepare their children to be marketable in a global world.[27]

Teachers' ability to innovate is harmed by this as well because they are expected to compete, but they are not at liberty to innovate and develop their product: the students.[28] Every teacher must teach the same or similar material to all of their students, and they have very little flexibility to adjust to their classroom's individual needs. The union encourages this model because competing factions would disrupt the monopoly, and uniformity is key for a government monopoly.

Teachers likely become frustrated by not being able to take control of their classrooms, have a say in which text books they should use, or the ability to spend more classroom time on one subject as opposed to another. These restrictions are imposed on them by inane laws and regulations. Former Mayor Goldsmith in the 1990s declared that it was futile to reform government schools because they are a monopoly, and the only way a monopoly can be reformed is through competition.[29]

Thus, this is why it is imperative that parents and students organize to insist on an all of the above smorgasbord approach to an educational model. It should include school vouchers, deregulated public schools, and more charter schools. The innovation of the competition will force innovation in the public sector, or else the public sector will fail in the market place. Without having someone monitoring and organizing on behalf of the parents, the only voice that will be heard is the teachers' unions.

A Start to Making Government Schools Competitive Again

There are three things that would put public schools back on track to compete internally and externally rather than to focus on thwarting competition: (1) realignment of teacher pay; (2) deregulation of teacher accreditation; and (3) reallocation of capital to our most needed investments.

1. Realign the teachers' pay incentives.

Like many government employees, teachers do not have incentive based pay. Incentive based pay is a flat salary coupled with the potential of making more money through bonuses based on one's performance. Thus, it is simply extra pay based on performance. Unlike other government bureaucrats, teachers have far more of a profound influence on the daily lives of constituents in their community than any other government official because the teachers' products are the future economic engine of the nation.

Incentive based pay and government service have generally been politically unpopular. Government employment is largely considered service to your local, state, or federal government on behalf of the community and/or nation. Thus, many have long been resistant to adopting pay models similar to the private sector. Incentive based pay for government employees also enables greater competition with the private workforce, and could lead to better delivery of governmental services. Incentives play to human beings innate self-serving nature. No matter how altruistic one is perceived, we all have a self-serving nature. If we are being rewarded for our hard work that goes above and beyond, then we are more likely to deliver on that "pledge" on a day-to-day basis because one will be compensated for it.

Similarly, the way American public schools recruits their teachers puts the country at a disadvantage. For example, public higher education institutions pay those who come from a professional discipline highly demanded in the private sector more than those who do not. By contrast, elementary and secondary educators' compensation is only increased based on seniority. It has nothing to do with one's performance, nor does it have anything to do with the knowledge that he or she brings to the classroom.[30]

For example, financial opportunities for math experts in the private sector are vast and lucrative, on average those working in that profession are paid higher wages on average. By contrast, English experts' opportunities are less lucrative and comparable to that of what one could make in the private sector.[31] It is not that people who work in fields that have more to do with language and arts aren't ever paid higher wages, it's that there is a larger disparity across the board. Thus, it would make sense to compensate individuals in a fashion that would make teaching more economically attractive for those subjects that are traditionally more technical and pay more outside the academic profession.

The ideal scenario would be to have a system that attracts more engineers, mathematicians, and statisticians to employment with primary and secondary schools. There is little incentive to do so if individuals in these specialized fields cannot make at least comparable pay to what they could make practicing their profession and not teaching it.

The goal is to attract the best math and science teachers and pay them at least a comparable wage. The labor market continually demands more mathematicians, computer programmers, engineers, and medical professionals. We need to recruit the very best and compensate them accordingly because their ability to produce and inspire students in the professions mentioned above is crucial to our economic sustainability and global competition. We will explore this even further in the next point having to do with teacher accreditation.

2. Deregulate state teacher accreditation requirements.

In Indiana, as in most states, to be an accredited teacher it requires at least a four year baccalaureate degree consisting of specified courses depending on the grade level one teaches. Secondly, as noted, there are different licenses based on the courses one took in his or her undergraduate studies that allows him or her to teach these grades. In sum, to teach in an Indiana elementary or secondary school you must have a degree in education and be licensed by the state. The license is not the main issue per se because most professional occupations require them to set standards about one's background and to regulate one's ethics, behavior, and to keep abreast with the best practices in his or her profession. At some point, however, some of these regulations should be revisited to see what is necessary and what is not.

For instance, why isn't the education degree waivable? Being a teacher is a unique talent, but I will say with confidence that lacking an education degree does not make a person unqualified to teach. In fact, there are people with education degrees who are not qualified to teach our students. In order to be a good teacher, one must be passionate, patient, inspirational, a leader, a commanding speaker, and have some sort of expertise at least when teaching a subject at the secondary level. These characteristics cannot be taught but describe a lot of people, most of whom are not teachers – at least by degree.

Former Federal Reserve Chairman, Alan Greenspan, writes:

> "[R]etirees or well-educated parents of students who volunteer to teach, part-time, courses such as math in which they have some proficiency are turned down because they lack a degree in education. To the extent that such practices are widespread, they are bureaucratic impediments to the functioning of market forces in education . . . ." [32]

Chairman Greenspan's point is that these people are some of the best minds in our communities and might want to find something to do to fill the void in their spare time. Moreover, these individuals in these fields have a comparative advantage with their subject matter because they specialize in it, know it well, will be able to convey the most crucial knowledge more efficiently, and have a passion for the field that may inspire students.

Something that always strikes me is that when high-profile politicians leave office they often get roles as professors, at least part-time at prestigious universities. Many of you can recall many former presidents and vice-presidents doing this at least on a part-time basis. Even their high-profile cabinet and staff members are afforded the same opportunities. The same is likely true for many governors across the country as well. These public servants usually have extensive backgrounds in business, law, and management. If they didn't have it before their service, they certainly acquired a thorough education in history, government, and politics during their tenure. Because of their experience in these areas, they can teach practical experience to students in higher education.

My point is that I can think of only one of our most recent former presidents who could teach in one of my local school communities if he wanted to post presidency: Lyndon B. Johnson. To my knowledge, he is the only one in recent history that had an education degree. Prior to his career in the United States Senate, the vice presidency, and then the presidency, he was a school teacher in Texas. By contrast, if former President Clinton wanted to spend the rest of his post presidency teaching high school government and political science at one of Indiana's local school communities, by law, he would not be qualified and would have to be turned away.

Many other retired and semi-retired professionals in their community would be turned away as well. There are a lot more of these types of people in our communities than there are former living presidents. These every day people may not have the celebrity of a former president, but many retirees and other professionals that wish to continue to work in their community are disqualified from teaching. My hunch is that no school district would say that these people are truly unqualified but those that represent the teachers, the unions, find it necessary to block the competition.

This is especially important in order for America to shore up its math deficiency. As mentioned, math based jobs are in demand, and, moreover, math is an integral foundation for science, medicine, and engineering. These are all jobs that pay decent wages, but America is simply not able to meet the market's demand. American teachers are not educating, or even interesting enough children in advanced math, science, and engineering.[33]

For example, as recent as 2000, 40% of secondary teachers that taught math did not have a major or minor in math, math education, or a related field.[34] As we will discuss math in the following chapters in greater detail, it has become more and more vital to American jobs, but a good number of individuals in the classroom who are teaching it are still learning it as well.[35] This might get the students by, but how could the 40% of secondary education teachers mentioned above relay the concepts underlying the method when they might not understand it either? As a matter of common sense, one cannot deny that this is a problem.[36]

Bringing "real world" experts into the primary and secondary classroom is important because too many high school graduates are lacking proficiency in math.[37] According to a study by the American Diplomatic Project, 62% of American entry-level jobs over the next ten years will require its workers to be proficient in algebra, geometry, data interpretation, probability, and statistics. Thus, students and parents must make sure that they are taking advanced courses and beginning them early.[38] Non-traditional educators have a proven record of success in the field, and they likely have a passion for it.

Moreover, they can demonstrate the real world uses of the importance of these foundations. In my experience, the ability for educators to relate concepts to the real world was something that was lacking at the primary and secondary education level, and it is a challenge still today. Most importantly, it may inspire more students to work harder in these areas, develop a passion for it, and turn the knowledge and skills that they learn into a sustainable career.

3. Reallocate resources and capital to our most needed resources.

As I will allude to in Chapter 4, more funding is not always the answer, but efficient use of the funding that a school already has, coupled with the freedom to distribute it to the best resources to maximize students' potentials is almost always the better answer. Nonetheless, it will take creative minds to find ways to reallocate the capital to make ends meet so that the tax dollars and investments in education are producing stronger results.

In fact, there are glimpses of this happening right here in Indiana. However, political leaders with progressive ideas on education must be supported. Otherwise, their ideas will go to the wayside and not come to fruition without political support.

On March 9, 2009, I read an article in the Indianapolis Star that made me proud of my state and gave me hope. Andy Gimmill from the *Indianapolis Star* wrote:

> "Six schools in the state have adopted the New Tech model, which uses technology as a cornerstone for learning and requires students to learn on their own in teams working on projects rather than listening to teachers lecture. Grades are based on portfolios created during those projects, as well as presentations and evaluations of team work."[39]

This policy is so important because it essentially outsources teaching to the most important life-long teacher one will have: themselves![40]

Moreover, it accomplishes real world experience because it encourages collaboration with teams, which is an ideal situation since most of these people will be doing exactly that in some way or another when they enter the workforce. This idea can be expanded further, and it needs to start by providing more students with computers and the Internet in their homes.

As a child, I remember President Clinton wanting to make it a priority before he left office that all public schools were connected to the Internet by the year 2000.[41] The nation came close to realizing that goal, but now the challenge is to connect every student's household to the Internet, which would also require that each child have access to a computer in the home. In fact, like most jobs today, a laptop should be part and parcel of a student's curriculum. This will have to be paid for primarily by reallocating capital that is distributed to outdated education policy, and put towards this goal of providing the Internet and computer access to each child's home.

For example, basics of English, spelling, and reading can be "outsourced" to the student. The teacher as the instructor can teach and inspire students how to question history, economics, and government, and write a thoughtful analysis or argument about a given subject. The point is that the student will be taking a larger role in instructing themselves through scripted lessons online. The students will be interacting with the material and practicing it rather than just listening and merely memorizing it. The teacher will then have more time to develop his or her true expertise and teach one what it means to think about the material creatively, make connections to the material to past events, and write about solutions on how to remedy or make things better.

Technology saves capital expenditures after one learns to use it efficiently. For example, what if the number of text books a student needs to thrive in the classroom was condensed, and their contents transferred to the computer, and reduced to practice problems. Effectively, it allows students to have access to the materials all year round, and to reference it as one progresses throughout their academic careers. This is a brief example of how reallocating capital spent on one resource might be transferred to invest and use as a tool in the modern classroom to fund more technologically based equipment.

Moreover, math and science problems are learned best through practice by doing these problems over and over until it clicks for the student. Also, the computer will be able to pinpoint where one made a mistake and why he or she made it, what he or she should've thought about to solve the problem, and what to look for with future problems. A learning portfolio can track the student and follow him or her throughout their academic career.

Technology should not ever replace the human teacher in the classroom because technology cannot sufficiently replace human interaction. Teachers are the governors of the classroom, and they are not there to reiterate what is in a book, but to relay to others creative ways to think about things. Connecting with a student in this way cannot be digitized and reduced to a computer program.

A final example that I will end this chapter with demonstrates much of the technology that we have already that is relatively cheap. Wouldn't it be convenient for a teacher's taped lectures and lessons to be posted and uploaded to the web? This would be convenient for those parents wanting to understand those math problems that they themselves have forgotten over time. However, pulling up his or her son or daughter's lecture would catch them up quickly and engage the parent in the classroom. Moreover, this is a form of accountability as well. The parents and teachers would be able to collaborate and have more transparency in the classroom. It would literally be a real-time demonstration of how the classroom works, which is of course one of my main points of this book.

The more parents understand how the classroom works, the better off his or her child will be. It will spark more interaction between the parent and child, and more collaboration between the teacher and the parent. We already have this technology; it is just needs to be put to use.

Consequences of Continued Union Domination

As we have seen, the current U.S. elementary and secondary education model has failed to prepare our children in this rapidly changing world for critical skills needed to be competitive in a global economy. Moreover, it has exacerbated the wage gap between skilled workers and non-skilled workers dramatically and disproportionately.[42] As legislatures across the world have tried many times, remedying a wage gap through legislation is not sustainable and effective in the long run, and in some cases many argue and statistics show that it merely drives unemployment up further.

As a result, it is time to go to the heart of the matter and arm young people with the individual skills they need to be competitive and put more middle-class students in higher skilled, higher wage earning careers to close the wage gap with free market based policies, increase our tax base, and have a wealthier more prosperous society. We can no longer ignore the fact that many unemployed workers will not find work easily. It is time to retrain them, and to start off right with the young so that economic downturns in the future will be mitigated, and America will have a competitive advantage on a skilled labor supply as we go farther into the twenty-first century.

Market Shortages

Failure to change this model will continue to devastate the most vulnerable. It will lead those marginalized without the chance for any of their talents to even begin to come to fruition, and those that could have entered a career that would have made a big difference in their earnings to be left stagnant in an underemployed position. By contrast, private schools and wealthier public schools are left less affected by this failure to change. Monetarily, they can afford to jump through the inefficient hoops erected by legislatures and bureaucrats via the unions and an outdated education model, and supplement the children's education with what they need to be competitive. Unlike wealthier school districts and private schools, average and below average funded schools barely satisfy the inane legal obligations set by regulation and statute by state legislatures and sometimes the federal government.

Because of the shortage of teachers with a solid background in math, science, and technology, it has produced nationwide shortages for careers that require that solid background in order to enter into as a young adult.[43] As mentioned, it is important for the teachers to have a solid basis for what they are teaching in the areas of math, science, and technology so that they can create a passion, and better yet maintain it with their students. This is important in middle-class and high risk areas especially because a student doesn't get to the more interesting courses until the higher level senior courses.[44] If you can't inspire passion and a strong understanding in the fundamentals, it is impossible to inspire a young man or woman to enter into a career that requires more study of the same basics at a higher and more complex level. Moreover, a poor understanding of the subject might disqualify them on the outset.

The American shortage of engineers, scientists, computer programmers, mathematicians, and medical doctors and other health professionals to name a few is more and more visible every day. Consequently, these professions are in high demand in America, and if you look around the younger professionals entering these fields are upper middle-class and foreigners transplanted to fill the void right here in America. This is a concrete example and proof of the disparate impact of wages among the middle-class and the upper middle-class and beyond.[45]

For example, in 1979, median compensation for college graduates was 38% higher than for high school graduates. Last year, that difference was 75%.[46] Policy makers who have affirmatively chosen to adhere to education policies of the past have forced far too many American workers deeper into commodization.[47]

Chapter 4: A Moral Hazard

"We are transforming our schools by raising standards and focusing on results. We are insisting on accountability, empowering parents and teachers, and making sure that local people are in charge of their schools . . . . . Challenging the soft bigotry of low expectations is the spirit of our education reform, and the commitment of our country: No child will be left behind."

President George W. Bush

Our current educational financial model is a moral hazard.

A moral hazard is not a reference to what is morally right or wrong per se, but an economic term to describe an economically irrational human behavior. The bigger the safety net is the greater the recklessness with which people, businesses, or government will tend to behave.[48] It is an economically irrational decision that under normal circumstances would be the wrong decision.

Rational consumers in general react to prices. When a good or service is in less demand, it is cheaper. In turn, demand for that good or service increases. When a good or service is in greater demand, it is more expensive and demand for that good or service tends to decrease after surpassing equilibrium. Price incentives are not effective any longer when a person encounters a good or service that is paid for by a third-party. Similarly, the same occurs when the cost is deferred until a later date such as with a loan where payments are deferred.

Generally, any industry primarily financed with public tax dollars and/or is heavily subsidized tends to be a moral hazard. This means, as stated earlier, our current educational financial model is a moral hazard. Another good example of an industry where a moral hazard is prevalent is healthcare.

The common denominator among these industries is they all have the illusion that someone else is paying for it, or it is free. As a result, individuals do not respond rationally because they operate under the false premise that the service is costless. Like anything else, there is nothing free about public education.

For example, students, who largely pay for their own higher education in this country, finance their education through school loans, scholarships, grants, or by a parent. These students are not forced to think of the costs contemporaneously with the purchase of the service, and they are less likely to consume with restraint, protest unjustified price increases, or demand fiscal discipline from the governmental entity that regulates or controls the industry. Thus, in higher education, most people as a result do not closely monitor the rising costs of education until after they begin repaying their loans.

Like most states, Indiana finances its public primary and secondary education through property tax levies from businesses, personal property, and residential property. If one is a homeowner, he or she often pays for their property taxes – regardless if they use the school system or not – via their mortgage. Again, this is a subtle but expensive purchase of a service, but no one pays too close of attention because it is another cost that is not contemporaneous with the purchase. These situations are always prone to runaway costs because individual psyches operate largely in the present. No one responds to it with market incentives unless there is a crisis.

For example, in Indiana, property tax caps were recently codified to limit the amount a local unit can levy against the property owner. However, it took a crisis for homeowners to protest and lobby their state legislatures. Older people who are many times on a fixed income were being squeezed tighter and tighter in order to afford to stay in their homes. Others were forced to sell their home because they could no longer afford the taxes. Urban flight to the suburbs was also an issue because the larger cities seemed to impose the larger property tax levies, but the urban areas statistically had the worst results in their education systems.

Not only did the 2007 through 2008 property tax crises prod the political majorities to demand change from their legislators and limit the burden on the taxpayer, but it also prompted other state leaders to shine light on the inefficiencies of the educational financing system, and once again highlight the poor results of many school districts. The true battle will be keeping the public engaged with this issue to gain the political support for education reform.

However, there will still be challenges in making sure that the money follows the individual students to improve the quality of education for each child. The following will look at how overhead and general administrative expenses can be reduced, and provide an example of a model that financially favors the student and is designed to produce results. Otherwise, the student can take his or her business elsewhere.

The Arms Race: How it Increases Overhead Expenses

Like an arms race between countries that compete to buy the best weaponry and technological defense, the education paradigm has an "arms race" as well. In education, this race is to continually purchase new facilities, textbooks, and other equipment. This problem largely stems from a mistaken belief that more government spending produces better results, and nowhere is this concept more entrenched than in education.[49] The arms race further complicates the issue. Like the misalignment of incentives for teachers' salaries, school districts compete for students not by meeting educational indicators and having a history of well-prepared students, but by providing lavish facilities and pristine sports complexes.

Namely, there is always the perception for the need for more money, but it is not always the solution for education reform and achieving results. Bureaucrats enable education administrators to purchase wildly without analyzing extensively what effect it will produce, if any, on the student. Of course some capital expenditures are worthwhile and very beneficial, but it is important to choose quality learning tools as opposed to mere marketing tools to attract more students to a district.

The financial model must be realigned to ensure the financial capital that is pumped into these schools for everything from new facilities, to high priced superintendents and administrators, to more efficient use of sporting facilities. As mentioned earlier, moral hazards often chill the amount of public interest in this issue unless there is an outward crisis because one does not consume educational services rationally as other goods and services in the free market.

Moreover, the constituents are often led to believe that more money will solve the problems in America's classrooms. Policy makers' primary solution is to push for further increases in state and federal budgets to provide more financial resources to school districts. However, this has not solved the problem. For example, Indiana invested $776 million extra in K-12 education over the past four years with no appreciable change in test scores.[50] This only further exemplifies the problem and provides a good example that the education financing model needs restructured.

Overhead

Administrative costs to operate school buildings have been highlighted several times during Governor Daniels' administration, and rightly so. During the 2009 legislative session Governor Daniels said, "Superintendent Bennett and I have submitted legislation to you to move tax dollars out of the back office and into the classroom; no one who obstructs that goal can claim to be an advocate of children learning." Before really analyzing the issue deeply, it made perfect sense to me from the beginning. This was not necessarily from a business standpoint but from personal experience—my primary and secondary education experience.

Without a doubt the two institutions I attended kept low overhead expenses. My grade school was founded in 1925 and was a relatively small structure that could hold approximately five hundred students, and I attended it from 1988 through 1996. By the time of my arrival, it had the original heating unit, no air-conditioning, almost all of the original structure, and a simple gymnasium for basketball and physical education. We shared Scecina High School's football field for other outdoor sports, which was just two city blocks east of the school.

During the months of August and September back in grade school the teacher would have to turn the lights off, and we worked from natural light, usually in the afternoons, because it was so hot that you stuck to your seat when you got up. My first couple years at high school were similar -- although the building had begun to be renovated after my arrival for additional classrooms. However, only the new addition was air conditioned at that time, and the old wing remained without it. Our sports teams did not suffer despite the presence of state of the art facilities. The discipline, coaching, and hard work earned many titles, and the rugged facilities might have even prepared some of the teams to survive in tough game time positions elsewhere.

The point of my story is not to suggest that newly built schools should not provide air conditioning, and children should be educated in a barn. It does demonstrate, however, that more can be done with less. In our case, our facilities were more dilapidated than our public peers, but neither our academic nor our athletic curriculums suffered. In fact, they exceeded our public counterparts on many different indicators across the board. Moreover, there was more efficient use of the facilities' spaces. Although during my grade school years energy was cheaper, I cannot say that these building were the most energy efficient. Now more than ever, it is critical that energy costs be contained in order to allow more money to flow to the classrooms and not the operation of the building.

Admittedly, even some of the poorer Catholic schools usually have some sort of private donations that enable the schools to finance many of their capital improvements. In my high school's case, it certainly benefited largely from alumni donations, and the deanery Catholic churches that support the Catholic Archdiocese high schools provide an enormous advantage that many public schools do not have. Nonetheless, the schools mentioned in my example still made capital improvements that it could afford for sustained operations.

As education reform takes hold, and more students receive quality education, the same pride in one's alma mater will likely develop over time. Thus, public-private foundations can be established to offset financing for capital improvements, and the efficient flow of money going into the classroom. This will take time, but it is doable. Moreover, state and local governments need to provide more attractive tax incentives so that wealthier individuals in the community can support their local school districts, especially at-risk school districts through private foundations.

Without a doubt, it is imperative that school districts adopt sustainable operational models to contain costs, and to allocate more money to each student. There is no longer any room for school districts that receive more money per student but have overhead costs that absorb much of that money before it ever reaches the student. Educators are in charge of a business, and it should be run more like one. In fact, educators are charged with producing society's most important product: human capital.

The next section will discuss one of the better—albeit likely the most controversial --- models that ensure that the dollars follow the student, and promotes efficiency and competition.

Vouchers

As indicated, the traditional educational financial paradigm plagues the elementary, secondary, and higher education institutions, and prevents far too many children from having capital follow and support students efficiently, and, accordingly, aids in failing to prepare students for higher education. Many have heard about "school choice" or "education vouchers," but too often this idea is tarnished and plagued with scare tactics and partisan politics driven by unions. In the meantime, great ideas such as these are pushed towards the wayside and the same ideas are pumped full of cash, but with the same or worse results than before.

A voucher is no more than a government bond issued to a citizen that has some sort of value in order to purchase a good or service, and the concept for school choice gained notoriety as early as the 1950s with the Nobel Prize winning economist Milton Friedman.[51] With school vouchers, it is a purchase of goods and services, and vouchers can and should be used to purchase educational services for the home that might further reduce the overhead costs for school districts across the nation.

The federal government proposed one of the largest school voucher programs most recently in 2005 after the catastrophic Hurricane Katrina devastating New Orleans, southern Mississippi, and parts of Texas. For example, New Orleans' school children still had to be educated, but much of the town was in ruins. In order for other school districts to absorb the displaced children in Louisiana all over the country, it only made sense to provide vouchers so that the school districts taking in the students could be compensated for their services.[52]

In "Googling" school choice or vouchers, I came up with the following common arguments both for against this policy initiative. Some of the arguments against a voucher policy include the following: vouchers will destroy public schools; kill qualified teachers' jobs; school choice is possible by other means; vouchers will decrease funding for already under funded urban schools; vouchers redeemed at parochial schools violate the constitution; and vouchers will discriminate against vulnerable classes of students.

By contrast, some of the popular arguments for vouchers are the following: vouchers will increase the quality of education; vouchers will promote economic diversity; vouchers will produce results and eliminate inefficiencies through creative destruction; and vouchers will reunite an education service with the consumer. There are likely many more, but these seemed to be the most common. Let's take a look at those arguments that are opposed to vouchers, and then those that are for it.

A. Opponents of Vouchers

1. *Vouchers will erode educational standards by diminishing the role of government oversight.*

The elimination of government oversight argument is in reference to lost governmental "oversight." A rational person would not argue that standards are not helpful for any institution whether it be public or private. In fact, some sort of bar or goal must be established for most anyone or any institution. As mentioned in Chapter 3, there is a fine line between establishing true standards, and merely providing over burdensome regulation to retain ultimate control. Once a good faith effort is established to figure out what is a standard and what is job protection and pure politics, this argument can be addressed.

Even if this is true, studies show that private schools outperform many of their public counterparts even if it is just marginally.[53] Moreover, private institutions are still subject to state standards if they desire to remain accredited, but they are freer to go beyond. Similarly, charter schools are public schools with less rigorous regulations, and have remained non-unionized thus far. Those that are performing well are in high demand, and those that are not will be and should be closed. The common denominators regarding educational success seem to be less oversight, more innovation, and the ability for the student to choose.

Finally, this argument misses the point regarding vouchers because by the very design of the policy it is supposed to create varied goals, standards, and ideas in order to compete for the optimal model. Thus, the regulations will be ceded to the individual schools and away from a "centralized government" model. Uniform standards should be established, but they should be thoughtful and for the advancement of education results.

2. *Vouchers will eliminate jobs.*

As addressed earlier in the book, the incentive based models for teacher performance needs to be revamped. Teachers that are performing their jobs poorly would be just as at risk as any other profession doing a poor job. A more competitive model would likely eliminate poor performing teachers, but I see nothing in the state constitution that gives a teacher with twenty plus years of teaching a right to a job.

However, there is a right to an education for all, and I think the majority of the citizens of this state could agree that this state right means a quality education. In any event, education reform should not be centered on job security for teachers, but instead it should focus on improved results for our students so that they may have a decent shot at being productive members of the global economy.

3. *School choice is possible by other means.*

The Indianapolis Public School system attempted this policy of an intra-district school choice program as opposed to general school choice. [54] The program allowed IPS students to choose a school outside of their assigned district. Prior to the program, students could only attend the school in the district they resided. It was a good attempt, and something that set the precedent for expansion. I applaud those that took the step and pushed for the reform. The right idea was certainly behind the decision: competition among the district schools.

However, like a restaurant franchise that is ultimately controlled by the same parent company that sets the standards, rules, guidelines, and menus, an intra-district school choice program does not go far enough because the school district is still the franchise equivalent of the franchising company. As a result, the school district is in ultimate control, and it is the school system that is the problem. [55] There were marginal differences between the same district schools. Some McDonalds may be preferred over others for taste and satisfaction, but ultimately they are almost entirely the same. It is no different with intra-district school choice.

4. Vouchers *decrease funding for already under funded schools.*

This arguments stems from the concept that students in a district who choose to attend another school or a private school leaves the school the student formerly attended with less money because that student is no longer present. This argument not only exacerbates the myth that education requires an endless amount of funding, but it also misses the entire point of a voucher system.

The *schools* performing poorly and not being chosen by parents and students in the education market place are not being under funded. The schools are underperforming for the student's needs. Indeed, it is important to have decent buildings and equipment to learn with, but vouchers are designed to fund the student, and pay for the expense that his or her presence costs the school district. We want schools to compete for the student by producing results for the kind of school it is conveying itself to be. The idea that the district should receive equal funding for all schools does not work, and it has killed innovation, and propped up poorly performing schools to their students' detriments.

5. *Vouchers violate the United States Constitution's Establishment Clause (separation of church and state).*

The First Amendment of the United States Constitution has many interpretations, and the First Amendment debate springs up quite often in education debates. Two common areas where the First Amendment establishment clause arises is in school sponsored prayer in public schools, and any time there is at least the perception that state or federal money is aiding a religious institution.

In this case, there is apprehension that if a student uses a voucher to attend a religious affiliated school, then the government has established a religious preference by providing money to a religious institution. Currently, the United States Supreme Court has held that in order for a voucher system not to violate the establishment clause it must pass a five part test: (1) the program must have a valid secular purpose; (2) the aid must go to the parents and not the schools; (3) a broad class of beneficiaries must be covered; (4) the program must be neutral with respect to religion; and (5) there must be adequate non-religious options.[36]

The late Chief Justice William Rhenquist of the United States Supreme Court wrote the following: "The incidental advancement of a religious mission, or the perceived endorsement of a religious message, is reasonably attributable to the individual aid recipients not the government, whose role ends with the disbursement of benefits."[57] This is currently the holding of valid case law regarding how a voucher system must be conducted in order to preserve the First Amendment.

A Supreme Court opinion does not of course preclude further disagreement. It is the law as it stands currently, however, and it deserves to be treated as such, and as long as the voucher system in a community follows and passes the five step analysis mentioned above, a voucher system should not be precluded.

6. *Vouchers will discriminate against vulnerable members of our society.*

There is a fear that students with behavior problems, learning disabilities, mental disabilities, and physical disabilities would be left behind and discriminated against and denied admission to private schools. Similarly, these classes of students would also lose out when competing to be granted admission to high performing public schools.

For example, the Indiana State Constitution provides for a blind and deaf school to accommodate these challenges. Children with disruptive behavioral challenges are often put into "alternative schools" where they can either learn skills to remedy their difficulties or remain in the "alternative school" until it is legal for them to not attend school. Also, developmentally challenged students are generally taught together because it maximizes teaching method efficiencies.

Physical disabilities are different in many respects, however. Although physical challenges by their very name are physical, there are many misconceptions and presumptions that these otherwise capable people are also challenged intellectually. This is of course not true, but the stigma makes these individuals vulnerable in the free marketplace. However, many private institutions would respond to the demand of the marketplace over time, and adapt facilities to meet the need or otherwise run the risk of losing voucher money, and, more importantly, lose a talented mind the school can tout as good will to attract new students. No doubt, a policy to mitigate the initial influx of facilities not designed to meet American with Disabilities Act standards will need to be put in place and implemented over time and tweaked until it is right.

B. Proponents of Vouchers

1. *Vouchers will increase the quality of education.*

Proponents of school vouchers point to the overall increase in the quality of education one receives because the school is competing for the students and tailoring their services to their needs. In turn, the student rewards the school with its presence via its voucher, and will likely remain a consumer at that school because the school's services are assisting the student in producing results to prepare him or her for future success. Competition forces an increase in the quality of an education, whereas in the current education paradigm the U.S. now offers, there is little incentive for improvement. The idea that education equality is providing a mediocre to poor education system for our students is misguided, and there is no wonder the U.S. is producing ill prepared students for college not to mention the global economy in general.

2. *Vouchers will promote economic diversity.*

The ability for a student to attend a school he or she otherwise would not be able to because of economic disadvantages is not only beneficial to that student, but also for those students that are situated in a stronger economic situation. To me, this is true education equality because socioeconomically disadvantaged students are able to attend an institution because of their intellectual abilities as a result of school choice. The school benefits, the student benefits, and the other students benefit from interacting with students outside their regular economic social groups. A child's glimpse of how the real world is made up is an education in itself.

3. *Vouchers will promote creative destruction.*

Some would be outraged that I would propose that a failing school be closed. However, I am outraged that failing schools are allowed to move forward and continue to put children at a long term disadvantage. Creative destruction is the natural destruction in a market that replaces the old goods or ways of providing a service with the new. For example, the horse and buggy went to the wayside as the Model-T car replaced it. I'm sure there were protectionists that advocated for the jobs that were destroyed in the horse in buggy industry, just as there are those that block new ways of providing educational services.[58] Educational methods and institutions that become outdated, ineffective, or obsolete should not be employed for the sake of bureaucratic protectionists. In the end, the students pay the price.

4. *Vouchers reunite the educational service supplier with the consumer.*

As mentioned, the state raises its revenue sources for education primarily through property taxes, and, in turn, appropriates the money to the school districts. The school district is charged with educating the child. A voucher structure appropriates the money to the student, and thus reunites the consumer with the service provider. This model encourages not only parents to get involved on the quality of service performed at the district level, but also those taxpayers who do not even have children, and for those whose children are already graduated from school.

Taxes

Although there will always be opponents that are convinced that property taxation is wrong, I think a reasonable and just property taxation system that is actually educating the students would be better taken. It allows those that are paying for other peoples' children to have a stake in the service because those children that become economic contributors to the community is one more independent person able and willing to provide for himself or herself for their future. In turn, that is one less person that is dependent indefinitely on someone else or the government.

Additionally, many complain that those parents already having the economic ability to pay for private schools will then be subsidized by the state. For example, The School Scholarship Tax Credit (STC) program will provide a 50% state tax credit for contributions made to qualified scholarship granting organizations (SGOs) which provide scholarships to low and middle income children to attend the private or public school of their choice.[59] The above concern is mitigated by having clear qualifying standards based on the federal poverty line.

Ideally, in a properly functioning education market no one would be precluded from receiving a voucher. I would argue that those not using the educational marketplace because they are without children or their children are past the age of primary and secondary education should still get a school voucher. This would keep the citizenry more engaged, and provide the political will for more people to demand better results because more will observe an ascertainable outcome of the tax dollars.

For example, individuals could donate their vouchers to create a financial pool to finance personal computers or subsidize Internet for those students without the financial means to buy the technological equipment or Internet service. In exchange, the donors should receive a tax credit. Also, reduced overhead costs and other savings created through more efficient methods would enable the possibility of providing Internet or community Wi-Fi Networks in order to outsource more education assignments and learning to the student in the home. The ideas are endless once the citizenry is engaged, placing input, and observing the results. The same or similar ideas should be put to work.

CHAPTER 5: STRAIGHT AHEAD, AS USUAL

"We know that education is everything to our children's future. We know that they will no longer just compete for good jobs with children from Indiana, but children from India and China and all over the world. We know the work and the studying and the level of education that requires."

President Barack H. Obama

The final scene of my favorite movie, *Scent of a Woman*, is an excellent lesson on leadership. This scene not only gives viewers encouragement to strive for integrity, but also it emphasizes that words versus actions are very different. In this scene, Lieutenant Colonel Frank Slade advocates vehemently on behalf of his young friend Charlie Simms, who is facing expulsion, before a disciplinary commission at an east coast, private boarding school.

Charlie received a scholarship to attend this very expensive boarding school where his acquaintances are heirs to large fortunes and legacies. At the beginning of the movie, Charlie witnessed vandalism with his wealthy classmate, George, where three of their mutual school mates concocted a scheme to vandalize the school's head master's brand new Jaguar, which had been presented to him by the board of trustees. The next day the stunt is pulled off, and the headmaster's new Jaguar is ruined with white paint. The headmaster stood by in humiliation, drenched with the paint, in front of the entire student body.

After the headmaster learns Charlie may know who caused him this embarrassment, the headmaster promises Charlie admission to Harvard in exchange for providing him with the vandals' identities. After Charlie's initial reluctance to provide the head master with this information, the headmaster gives Charlie the four day Thanksgiving weekend to think about his decision. Unlike the three vandals and

George who were off to an extravagant ski trip for Thanksgiving, Charlie stayed behind in town to aid a blind retired colonel in order to earn plane fare home for Christmas. Charlie is supposed to assist Lt. Col. Frank Slade at his home in the quaint New England town, but instead, to Charlie's surprise, he is whisked off to New York City for a four day education of a lifetime.

At the end of the film, Col. Slade's driver drops Charlie off at his dorm after their trip to New York so he can prepare for his hearing before the joint student-faculty disciplinary commission. He is surprised when Col. Slade joins him at this hearing. After the headmaster presses hard for information about the incident prior to Thanksgiving break, Charlie refuses to provide the vandals' names in exchange for his Harvard education. His cohort, George, appears at the hearing with his wealthy father, a notable alumnus of the school. In the end, George provides the headmaster with the vandals' identity but blames his eyesight for the vagueness and casts doubt on his own testimony. His intent was clearly to punt the conclusive identification to Charlie, but Charlie sticks to his principles and refuses to sell someone out just to buy his future. The head master recommends expelling Charlie for his failure to cooperate, and praises George for showing pride in continuing his family's legacy at the elite institution.

Col. Slade strongly objects and delivers a riveting speech on leadership, integrity, and actions versus words. A blunt line from Col. Slade's speech says in part, "When the [****] hits the fan, some guys run, and some guys stay. Here's Charlie facing the fire, and there's George hiding in big daddy's pocket. And what are you going to do? Reward George and destroy Charlie."[60]

For too long, there have been leaders not willing to face the fire occurring within our educational system. As a result, we have too many unskilled workers that are underemployed or unemployable. When the pressure increases from competing interests with regard to education reform, too many people run. We need more to stay and face the fire. In this final chapter we'll look at why leaders for this cause are so important, and why it is vital to publicly support their actions and hold them accountable to their words.

Finally, I will offer some suggestions and other initiatives, some of which have been tried elsewhere, to spark true reform. As you have read thus far, there are a lot of distractions and a lot of red tape that hide the ball. It is imperative, now more than ever, that we keep our eye on the finish line and stick with the most efficient route. Our focus must be on improving students' vital educational benchmarks, raising standards, and measuring results. Finally, I'll set forth the charge to move forward towards success.

Leaders

At times, political leaders have the duty to convince their constituencies conventional wisdom is just plain wrong. Those leaders that refuse to do this – especially on important policies like education – are followers.[61] To advance education reform, I believe we need more political, business, and civic leaders like Governor Mitch Daniels, Indiana Superintendent of Public Instruction Tony Bennett, former Indianapolis Mayor Bart Peterson, and New York City Mayor Michael Bloomberg, to name a few. These folks produce action versus words, even in states and communities where the opposing factions are just as strong and active as in other areas of the country. The common themes of these leaders' policies with regard to education are centered on results, not on a rigid bureaucratic structure.

Glimpse of the Status Quo: Words vs. Acts

Shortly after the presidential inauguration on January 20, 2009, and about a quarter of the way into the year, current U.S. Education Secretary Arne Duncan visited New York City. During this visit, Duncan spoke up for charter schools and mayoral control of education. The Wall Street Journal reported that this was the reformer talking. Behind the scenes, the Obama administration allowed Congress to kill a District of Columbia voucher program even as Mr. Duncan was sitting on evidence of its success according to the Wall Street Journal.[62]

"[W]hile running for President last year, Mr. Obama told the Milwaukee Journal-Sentinel that if he saw more proof that they [vouchers] were successful, he would 'not allow my predisposition to stand in the way of making sure that our kids can learn . . . You do what works for the kids.'"[63] The Wall Street Journal went to say that the President should've qualified his statement with: "Except, apparently, when what works is opposed by unions."

The voucher program that was touted as being widely successful was called the Opportunity Scholarship Program. This program provided $7,500.00 vouchers to 1,700 low-income families in the District of Columbia to send their children to private schools. Ninety-nine percent of the applicants were African-American or Hispanic, and there were more than four applicants for each scholarship.[64] The political pressure from the teachers' unions forced the administration to pull the plug on a program working for disadvantaged children in its own back yard.

The Wall Street Journal described Congress' decision to let 1,700 poor kids get tossed from private school as a moral disgrace. It exposed the ugly politics that lies beneath union and liberal efforts across the country to undermine mayoral control, charter schools, vouchers or any reform that threatens union monopoly over public education dollars and jobs.[65] I agree wholeheartedly that this is a moral disgrace. It is unclear what deal the Administration had to cut, or strategically why it chose to forgo this voucher program. Nonetheless, this is a prime example of why mayoral control at the local level would level the playing field at the state legislatures and perhaps mayors collectively across the United States with similar interests could organize and provide balance to the debate in Washington, D.C.

With this glaring example said, the administration is still new. It would be unfair and unwise to judge its education policy too harshly for now. This does not seem promising and is convincing evidence, however, as to why we need someone representing the parents and students. This presidential administration has the political weight to bring about education reform because of its historical significance and general popularity. Moreover, the Obama administration has the credibility to reshape the debate regarding education reform, and cast it legitimately as the new civil rights movement.

It is the new civil rights movement because more minorities and socio-economically disadvantaged youth need an educational model that prepares them for the workforce. Children of all colors and socioeconomic backgrounds deserve school choice, and to be armed with the skills they need to qualify for jobs after they are done with school that are sustainable and less likely to be automated or outsourced. These groups need a policy that helps them from the beginning of their education and not just affirmative action type policies designed to "catch these groups up" after they graduate high school.

Perhaps I unfairly turn the heat up on Democratic politicians with regard to education policy, but realistically Democrats have a stronger relationship with the teachers' unions and a long history with them. With that said, sometimes certain parties are just able to get certain policies advanced easier than others. I don't care who reforms our education policy, and neither does the majority of all Americans. But we can all agree now is the time to get a move on with reform.

Transfer to Local Control

As mentioned earlier in the book, school districts are controlled by local school boards. However, with all due respect to many of these individuals' services, they have little to no accountability – at least to the voters anyway. If you recall, they are elected during an election primary. This is when the members of the major parties go to the ballot and elect their nominees, but it also has an extremely low voter turnout. Of the 20-30% of the registered electorate that go to the polls during this spring day in Indiana, these people are largely focused on the party nominees. In truth, the only way to enact education reform is to first hold someone solely accountable for it at the local level. The most visible person in a community accountable to local voters and has lobbyists working on behalf of his or her administration is the mayor of a city.

This idea worked in New York City when Mayor Michael Bloomberg won the right to appoint the majority of the school board and gained control over policy. Bloomberg could set the general direction of the system because he and the chancellor shared the system.[66] The results were positive. With New York City's 1.1 million students, mayoral control resulted in better test scores and graduation rates, while expanding charter schools that led to better education choices for low-income families.[67] Similarly, Secretary of Education Arne Duncan advocates for turning control of Detroit's school system over to the mayor, and Duncan has stated he is encouraged by Mayor Bing's interest in Detroit Schools.[68]

Arguably, Detroit has one of the most decrepit schools systems in the country, and it is in desperate need for reform. It is imperative that this city enact constructive changes for school reform at the ground level. The automotive jobs that used to thrive there are no longer reliable.

Detroit must, through education reform, give these young men and women opportunities to succeed in other ventures by equipping the students with the tools to succeed.

One of the most notable gains in turning over education reform to mayoral control would be the ability of the mayoral administration to lobby for tools to produce results in education and not jobs at the state legislature. This would balance the debate at the legislative level and dilute the teachers' unions' monopoly over education policy. For example, after a mayor gains control of the local school district's boards, he or she could implement his or her policies through a full-time local education department at the city level. The better the success at the local levels, the harder it is for the state legislature to cast legislative change requests to the side if clear evidence of success is provided.

Getting mayoral control would be the fight of a lifetime. Mayor Bloomberg and other mayors did not get mayoral control indefinitely but with sunset provisions, meaning that control expires and must be renewed by the New York State legislature. Each time this mayoral initiative runs the risk of being diluted or taken away altogether depending on the political winds at the state legislature.[69] Nonetheless, it is a fight worth fighting, and one that is worth continuing to fight. A proven result only makes it harder for the opposition to make their argument.

The Parents' Union

In order for a mayor to gain control of his or her school district, mayors are going to need parents united behind them. Although most of these families can't provide financial contributions to lobby these state representatives and senators, they can organize in constructive ways to make their voices heard at the state house. We live in an age where social networking sites dominate many aspects of public relations. In our busy and fast paced society, you can organize and also stay informed with quick briefings of different policies that might benefit your school district.

Organizing on social networking sites, like Facebook, enables parents to share ideas, unite together, and enables them to do it conveniently. Similarly, joining the Indiana Department of Education's page or U.S. Department of Education's page on these same sites enables one to be briefed on upcoming initiatives. Parents can decide to read into it further if it sparks their interest or if they think it is worthy of a harder look. Also, many of your state representatives and senators are also members of these social networking sites. It is an easy way for their staffs to communicate with different groups as well, and for them to gauge your interest in a particular issue.

When communicating with these elected officials, it is important to always write constructive letters whether criticizing or supporting a public servant's initiative. Not only does this give a constituent credibility, but also it implicitly shows that you are a constituent and to pay attention to you because you are informed and want your child to have the very best education in exchange for your hard earned tax dollars. In order for a democracy to truly be functional, the public servants must have your support in order to counter special interests. For those of you that say that you are happy with the status quo, or that politics don't matter because it is all the same anyway, I would hope you would feel differently by now, at least, when it comes to education reform.

What Local Communities Can Do Now

Over the past six years, I have volunteered in reading programs in both Monroe County and Marion County, Indiana. It was a fulfilling experience, and I recommend to any of you to volunteer your time to help a student read. The one thing I would often think about on my way to tutor or on my way back is why there is isn't more math and science programs that individuals could volunteer to assist with in their local community school systems. Reading is of course absolutely paramount to any sort of success or progress academically and economically in the future. However, as I've noted, math and science skills are drastically on the decline in the United States, and many parents could use a quick brush up on these skills as much as their children need them.

This is important because throughout my life I have too often heard individuals say that they can't do math, they've tried and tried but just don't get it. They don't like math. Math terrifies them and they freeze up and cannot move through an exam or problem. In worse cases, I have heard parents say this in front of their children. In my opinion, when a parent shows a lack of confidence or a fear, it is passed onto a child. In turn, that child has been set back unnecessarily for his or her math studies. I add science courses into this as well because many of the advanced sciences are based on math skills.

To combat this problem, local communities need to organize their math whizzes and encourage them and provide incentives to tutor in the classrooms. This will provide a refresher to those that are behind, reinforce these skills for those that are almost there but the concept still has not quite clicked yet, and inspire more to pursue math based careers after being encouraged and having their confidence strengthened.

Strengthening and Continuing What Works: Charter Schools

Former Indianapolis Mayor Bart Peterson secured the ability from the legislature to grant charters for a charter school system in Indianapolis in 2001.[70] A key component of this Charter School Initiative was the former mayor's unique position of direct accountability to all city residents, unlike superintendents or school committee members.[71] After a proven success, Peterson's successor, Mayor Greg Ballard, vowed to continue this policy and has become a strong advocate for it himself. A charter school, while part of the public system, is free to experiment with innovative teaching and learning methods that may or may not be consistent with school district guidelines.[72]

School districts are supposed to judge charter schools on results, extending the charter if children show improved educational performance, revoking it if they don't.[73] Teachers, parents, and students sign a compact of commitment to their respective roles and students recite a "code of respect" that reflects the school's special rules. Teachers and administrators are on yearly contract with no tenure, but get bonuses for meeting or exceeding performance.[74]

By now, you can see why this sounds like a good idea. It sounds like what I have been writing about: a deregulated school based on innovation and results. Unions have tried to cap the number of charter schools in a state, get rid of them entirely, discredit them, and a whole host other tactics to quash the competition that these schools give to their traditional public counter parts. Instead, the traditional public schools should adopt similar policies, and innovate their own ideas to compete against the charter schools. Traditional public schools prohibit this innovation, however.

Two famous athletes have sponsored their own charter schools around the country: Tiger Woods and Andre Agassi. Mr. Agassi's school caps the class size, which is said to be helpful in increasing the quality of what a student learns. Also, his school lasts two hours longer each day, and the school year is ten days longer than traditional counterparts. Longer hours and longer school years are beginning to take hold across the country as a way to have our students increase competition globally, and it needs to be encouraged throughout all districts. The United States spends much less time in school per day and over the year than most other industrialized nations.[75]

Similarly, Mr. Woods' school emphasizes some of the inspirational techniques I have mentioned previously in this book in order to attract students to practical knowledge that will be used in an actual sustainable and well paying careers. Young people in his school have a chance to go beyond their normal classroom work with unique enrichment programs that include forensic science, engineering, aerospace, video production, and home design. These are wonderful ways to inspire a student to enter one of these fields and to intrigue them early.[76] Also, it should be noted that these are careers in high demand, and ones that are harder to be shipped abroad or automated.

In an age when many of our popular culture stars and athletes misbehave and set less than impressive examples to the thousands of children who look up to them, these two athletes should be recognized for their excellence in education reform and leadership[1]. Similarly, it is a strong message that academics should be first in a student's life and athletics second.

There is strong evidence that where charter schools are present they are largely working, and if not they are closed just like other failing systems. Economist Tim Sass and colleagues found that middle-school students at charters in Florida and Chicago who continued into charter high schools were significantly more likely to graduate and go on to college than their peers who returned to district high schools because charter high schools were not available.[77] I am not saying that this is conclusive evidence of a national model, but it is indicative that the

---

1   Mr. Agassi still deserves recognition for his sponsorship of this school despite his recent acknowledgement of illicit drug use back in 1997. Likewise, when going through the final rewrite of this book, Mr. Woods' public image took a turn for the worse. It is still my opinion that both of their efforts in promoting educational opportunities for young children should be noted.

states endorsing charter schools are onto something. These charters need to be protected and not destroyed for political reasons, i.e. bills introduced into the legislature that impose caps on the number of charter schools that can be established in states.

As Parents, Students, and Patriots
We Approve the Following Message

All of us being privileged to live in the information age, we are given a great advantage over many generations because we can be our *own* investigative journalists. With that said, one needs to know how to "filter" credible sources from junk on the Internet, newspapers, television, and radio. One should continually ask how one arrived at his or her statistics and scrutinize his or her answers, differentiate fact from opinion, gather both sides of an issue, and finally arrive at one's own informed opinion. Regardless of the perception that the twenty-four hour news cycle or other news outlets portrays that they are infallible and unbiased. One cannot arrive at an informed opinion through sound bites and blind trust, alone, regarding our sacred fourth branch of government: the media.

There is a lot of *stuff* out there, and a lot of people who put this stuff out there do not leak it by mistake. It is leaked to confuse and mask. There seems to be a strong consensus that many citizens are very tired of being talked to instead of listened to. As I have tried to reveal, in order to really increase political power on an issue, it is vital to organize constructively, peacefully, and support the leaders that are not afraid of breaking away from the conventional wisdom or perceptions that are meant to consciously mislead citizens.

Without a doubt, we all want an educational model that prepares students for a sustainable career and provides them with skills to be self-sufficient so that they can be productive members of our local, state, and national economies. More importantly, more students need to graduate with a sense of self-worth, confidence, and duty to contribute and leave their community better than they found it. The difference is that there are varying factions in this debate that have very different ways at arriving at this end goal.

My suggestions are not perfect or novel, but the main point is that they are unconventional. I think that we can build consensus on the idea that the conventional education model is no longer effective, and it is going to cost us and our children big in the long-run. In fact, it has already cost us greatly in socio-economically disadvantaged neighborhoods and communities. As I have relayed, there are far too many of these kids being left behind not because of an intellectual incapacity but because of a system that fails them and breeds a vicious cycle.

In sum, let's not lose sight of our end goal: preparing our children for a global economy, and providing sustainable skills that are less likely to be outsourced or automated. The challenge will be enormous, and the roadblocks will be stronger than ever. There will be varying factions erecting obstacles to create distractions. It reminds me of when I was a child being exposed to the outside world and its complexities for the first time, and being easily distracted and constantly told to move along in order to get all that we needed to get done in just a few short hours of a day.

Irony is when a smart aleck phrase becomes a lifelong lesson. My simple motto kept me on the right course and enabled me to not lose sight of what I was striving to achieve. I intend to keep it. Similarly, public policy debates are a vacuum filled with all sorts of falsehoods, scare tactics, biases, media sound bites without context, biased coverage, and other tactics designed to create confusion that in turn creates inaction. It is designed to wear down members of the public that do not have the time or resources to devote to a very active debate. As a result, it leaves far too many people in the middle confused and distracted from what works, and what does not work, and what other alternatives there are to remedy education.

In the end, there are three things to keep in mind before beginning this journey. Take a hard look at what models are producing results and how the statisticians arrived at those statistics. Two, the ultimate goal of our education model is to produce well prepared children for productive, rewarding, and sustainable careers. Three, the education reform debate will be filled with all sorts of tactics to get the majority of the people who have to live with these policies that were like my family off the right road, and lead them down the wrong one.

The ideas of local control, vouchers, charter schools, and deregulating traditional public schools are not novel. The tools to implement these policies have always been there lying at the end of the road waiting for the programs to be implemented on a wide scale. Indeed all of these models need to be used contemporaneously with each other to create a synergy, eliminate inefficiencies, and maximize strengths. By now, there's no doubt that the path to solid reform is no different than the path to any other American goal taught to us by many that have gone before us designed to make us a more prosperous nation. Do not be distracted by the tactics of those attempting to obstruct freedom from oppressive government systems, just keep moving straight ahead, as usual.

ENDNOTES

1   Alan Greenspan, *The Age of Turbulence: Adventures in a New World*. New York: The Penguin Press, 2007: 403.

2   Thomas L. Friedman, *The World is Flat*. New York: First Picador Edition, 2007: 537

3   http://www.faniq.com/blog/Video-Michael-Phelps-Jason-Lezak-And-USA-4x100-Freestyle-Relay-Team-Beat-France-To-Win-Gold-Blog-10943

4   Steven D. Levitt & Stephen J. Dubner, *Freakonomics: A Rogue Economist Explores the Hidden Side of Everything*. New York: HarperCollins, 2005: 161.

5   Nicholas Kristof, "How to Raise Our I.Q." *New York Times* 15 April 2009.

6   Ibid.

7   Friedman, 361.

8   Friedman, 378.

9   Friedman, 136.

10 Friedman, 279.

11 Friedman, 280.

12 Friedman, 286.

13 Friedman, 345.

14 Friedman, 344.

15 Friedman, 381.

16 Bill Clinton, *My Life*. New York: Vintage Books Edition, 2005: 308.

17 Friedman, 395.

18 Tom Brokaw, *The Greatest Generation*. New York: Random House, 1998: 212.

19 Friedman, 359.

20 Friedman, 48.

21 Stephen Goldsmith, *The Twenty First Century City: Resurrecting Urban America*, Washington, D.C.: Regency Publishing, Inc., 1997: 123.

22 Vic Ryackaert, "IPS Approves Layoffs of 300 Teachers." *The Indianapolis Star*, 28 April 2009.

23 Ibid.

[24] Goldsmith, 115.

[25] Goldsmith, 116.

[26] Goldsmith, 118.

[27] David Dranove, *The Economic Revolution of American Healthcare.* Princeton, New Jersey: Princeton University Press, 2000: 8-10.

[28] Goldsmith, 120.

[29] Goldsmith, 115.

[30] Greenspan, 404.

[31] Greenspan, 405.

[32] Greenspan, 405.

[33] Friedman, 349.

[34] Greenspan, 462.

[35] Greenspan, 462.

[36] Greenspan, 462.

[37] Greenspan, 404.

[38] Friedman, 302.

[39] Gimmill, Andy, High School May Be in For Big Changes, Indianapolis *Star,* March 9, 2009.

[40] Friedman, 309-10.

[41] *My Life,* 597.

[42] Greenspan, 505.

[43] Bill Clinton, *Giving: How Each of Us Can Change the World.* New York: Knopf, Borzi Books, 2007: 76.

[44] Friedman, 352.

[45] Greenspan, 398.

[46] Friedman, 284.

[47] Friedman, 14-15.

[48] Greenspan, 189.

[49] Goldsmith, 121.

[50] Neal, Andrea., http://teamhammondtaxpayersgroup.blogspot.com/2008_12_28_archive.html, January 1, 2009.

[51] Milton Friedman, "Vol. 6 – What's Wrong with Our Schools," *IdeaChannel.tv,* 1980. IdeaChannel. <http://www.ideachannel.tv/>

[52] Amy Goldstein, "Bush Proposes Vouchers for All Displaced Students," *Washington Post,* 20 Sept. 2005.

[53] Goldsmith, 113.

[54] Goldsmith, 119.

[55] George Shultz, *Turmoil and Triumph: My Years as Secretary of State.* New York: Charles Scribner's Sons, 1993: 1081.

[56] *Zelman vs. Simmons-Harris,* 536 U.S. 639 (2002).

[57] Ibid.

58 Greenspan, 48-51.

59 School Choice Indiana, "Indiana School Scholarship Tax Credit,"*School Choice Indiana*. 2009 http://www.inscholarshiptaxcredit.com/.

60 *Scent of a Woman*. Prod. Martin Brest. Dir. Martin Brest. Perf. Al Pacino and Chris O'Donnell. DVD. Universal Studios, 1992

61 Greenspan, 462.

62 Editorial, *"Democrats and Poor Kids: Sitting on Evidence of Voucher Success, and the Battle of New York." Wall Street Journal*, 6 April 2009.

63 Ibid.

64 Ibid.

65 Ibid.

66 Rudolph W. Giuliani, *Leadership*. New York: Hypersion, 2002: 175.

67 *Democrats and Poor Kids.*

68 Corey Williams, "Education Secretary: Detroit Schools 'Ground Zero,'" Washington *Post*, 13 May 2009.

69 *Democrats and Poor Kids.*

70 "Mayor's Charter Schools Initiative," Government Innovators Network, 2006 http://www.innovations.harvard.edu/awards.html?id=48911.

71 Ibid.

72 *Giving*, 74.

73 *Giving*, 74.

74 *Giving*, 74-75.

75 *Giving*,74.

76 *Giving*, 76.

77 Jay P. Green, "The Union War on Charter Schools, As New York Shows, They Want to Kill Any Education Choice," *The Wall Street Journal*, 16 April 2009.